EXPLORING THE STATES

Florida

THE SUNSHINE STATE

by Emily Rose Oachs

BLASTOFF! READERS
5

BELLWETHER MEDIA · MINNEAPOLIS, MN

Note to Librarians, Teachers, and Parents:

Blastoff! Readers are carefully developed by literacy experts and combine standards-based content with developmentally appropriate text.

Level 1 provides the most support through repetition of high-frequency words, light text, predictable sentence patterns, and strong visual support.

Level 2 offers early readers a bit more challenge through varied simple sentences, increased text load, and less repetition of high-frequency words.

Level 3 advances early-fluent readers toward fluency through increased text and concept load, less reliance on visuals, longer sentences, and more literary language.

Level 4 builds reading stamina by providing more text per page, increased use of punctuation, greater variation in sentence patterns, and increasingly challenging vocabulary.

Level 5 encourages children to move from "learning to read" to "reading to learn" by providing even more text, varied writing styles, and less familiar topics.

Whichever book is right for your reader, Blastoff! Readers are the perfect books to build confidence and encourage a love of reading that will last a lifetime!

This edition first published in 2014 by Bellwether Media, Inc.

No part of this publication may be reproduced in whole or in part without written permission of the publisher. For information regarding permission, write to Bellwether Media, Inc., Attention: Permissions Department, 5357 Penn Avenue South, Minneapolis, MN 55419.

Library of Congress Cataloging-in-Publication Data

Oachs, Emily Rose.
  Florida / by Emily Rose Oachs.
    pages cm. – (Blastoff! readers. Exploring the states)
  Includes bibliographical references and index.
  Summary: "Developed by literacy experts for students in grades three through seven, this book introduces young readers to the geography and culture of Florida"– Provided by publisher.
  ISBN 978-1-62617-008-7 (hardcover : alk. paper)
  1. Florida–Juvenile literature. I. Title.
  F311.3.O23 2014
  975.9–dc23
                                                                              2013004331

Printed in the United States of America, North Mankato, MN.

Table of Contents

Where Is Florida?

Florida is a narrow **peninsula** in the southeastern United States. It is the nation's southernmost state on the mainland. Only Hawaii stretches farther south. The Atlantic Ocean lies to the east and south of Florida. To the west is the **Gulf** of Mexico. Alabama and Georgia border Florida's **panhandle** in the north. The capital city of Tallahassee is located in this narrow stretch of land.

An **archipelago** called the Florida Keys curves around the southern tip of the Florida peninsula. This island chain lies along the Florida **Straits**. One of the islands is Key West. It sits about 90 miles (145 kilometers) north of Cuba.

South
Carolina

Georgia

Atlantic
Ocean

• Jacksonville

★ Tallahassee

Florida

Gulf of
Mexico

• Tampa

Everglades
National Park

Miami

Florida Keys

Key West

Florida Straits

History

The Apalachee, Calusa, Timucua, and other **Native Americans** were the first to live in Florida. Spanish explorer Juan Ponce de León and other Europeans reached the peninsula during the 1500s. In 1821, the United States gained control of Florida. Florida became a state in 1845. In 1861, the state fought for the **Confederacy** during the **Civil War**.

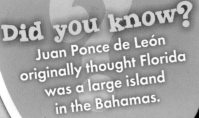

Did you know?
Juan Ponce de León originally thought Florida was a large island in the Bahamas.

Florida Timeline!

1513:	Spanish explorer Juan Ponce de León lands in Florida and claims it for Spain.
1817-1858:	Three periods of war occur between the United States and the Seminoles.
1821:	The United States officially gains control of Florida from Spain.
1845:	Florida becomes the twenty-seventh state.
1861:	Florida withdraws from the United States to fight for the Confederacy in the Civil War.
1868:	Florida rejoins the United States.
1960s:	Many Cubans move to Florida because they are unhappy with their government.
1969:	The Kennedy Space Center in Cape Canaveral sends the first person to the moon.
1971:	Walt Disney World opens in Orlando.
2010:	The Gulf of Mexico oil spill harms Florida wildlife.

Seminole wars

first moon landing

Walt Disney World opening

The Land

Florida Keys

sinkhole

fun fact

In some parts of Florida, water wears away rock under the soil. Eventually, the rock caves in to create massive sinkholes.

Florida is a low-lying state. Its highest point, Britton Hill, is only 345 feet (105 meters) above sea level. Forested, hilly land covers the panhandle and central Florida. Along the state's eastern and western coasts are rolling **plains**. Sandy beaches of many colors meet the ocean waters.

Did you know?
Hurricanes often strike Florida in summer and fall. These violent storms bring strong winds and heavy rain to coastal areas.

Florida's Climate
average °F

spring
Low: 61°
High: 81°

summer
Low: 73°
High: 90°

fall
Low: 65°
High: 83°

winter
Low: 51°
High: 70°

The large Lake Okeechobee sits in south-central Florida. Big Cypress Swamp, the Everglades, and other wetlands stretch south from this lake. In the far south, limestone and **coral** form the Florida Keys. Florida's **subtropical** climate means the state is usually warm and humid. Coastal breezes help cool the mainland during hot summers.

The Everglades

The Everglades is an area of wetlands in southern Florida. It is a shallow, slow-moving river. Usually the water is no deeper than 12 inches (30 centimeters). Tall **saw grass** grows from the water in the north. In the south, water flows through swamps and salty **marshes**.

In the early 1900s, people were draining the Everglades for farmland. Writer Marjory Stoneman Douglas worked hard to stop this. Many rare animals live in this region. She wanted to save their home. In 1947, Everglades National Park was established. This preserved part of Florida's unique wetlands.

fun fact !

During the 1800s, some Seminoles hid in the Everglades to keep their land and avoid capture.

Seminoles

Everglades National Park

Wildlife

alligator

Did you know?
Florida is home to the coral snake, rattlesnake, water moccasin, and copperhead. These are all of the venomous snakes found in the U.S. In all, more than 40 different types of snakes live in the state.

Florida is home to many **endangered** animals. The Key deer can only be found in the Florida Keys. This tiny deer stands under 3 feet (0.9 meters) tall. In the south, the rare Florida panther stalks its prey in woods and swamps. Alligators lurk in Florida's rivers and wetlands. In the Everglades, American crocodiles also bask in the sun.

Key deer

water moccasin

manatee

Manatees, also known as sea cows, weigh up to 1,000 pounds (454 kilograms). These massive mammals somersault and roll through the sea. Giant manta rays swim beside **coral reefs**. Black skimmers fly low over the ocean's surface to scoop up fish. Spoonbills wade through marshes to catch their dinners.

Landmarks

Florida is full of fun and historical landmarks. Walt Disney World is among the most-visited **tourist** sites in the world. This Orlando theme park has rides and other attractions based on Disney's imaginative stories. Tampa Bay's Busch Gardens is a unique mix of zoo and amusement park. In a single day, visitors can ride roller coasters and see African animals.

Visitors learn about the history of space exploration at Cape Canaveral's John F. Kennedy Space Center. Space shuttles to the moon were once launched from this site. In Saint Augustine, people explore the magnificent Castillo de San Marcos. Spanish settlers built this fortress over 300 years ago!

John F. Kennedy Space Center

Castillo de San Marcos

Walt Disney World

Miami sits at the mouth of the Miami River on Biscayne Bay. It is the second largest city in Florida. Two out of every three people who live in Miami have roots in Latin or South America. In some areas, more people speak Spanish than English. Many companies that work with Latin America have headquarters here.

Miami Beach

Miami Beach is an island in Biscayne Bay. It separates the city of Miami from the Atlantic Ocean. This 10-mile (16-kilometer) long island is famous for its many **resorts**. Tourists are drawn to its beautiful beaches, tropical plants, and warm weather.

Working

Did you know?
Millions of older Floridians no longer work. They moved to the state after retiring. They want to enjoy Florida's warm, sunny climate.

18

Almost nine out of every ten workers in Florida have **service jobs**. Many people have jobs in tourism. They work at hotels, restaurants, and resorts. Factory workers build computers and other electronics. Farmers harvest sugarcane and vegetables. Their cows graze on Florida's western grasslands. Fishers catch crabs, snappers, and lobsters in the coastal waters.

Florida is famous for its oranges. The state also produces grapefruits and tangerines. These **citrus fruits** grow in **groves** in southern Florida. Most of the country's orange juice is processed in the state.

Where People Work in Florida

manufacturing
4%

farming and
natural resources
1%

government
12%

services
83%

Playing

Floridians like to support their sports teams. They sit courtside to watch the Orlando Magic or Miami Heat dunk on the basketball court. Fans of professional football root for the Miami Dolphins, Tampa Bay Buccaneers, or Jacksonville Jaguars. Many professional baseball teams travel to Florida for spring training each year.

Racing fans flock to the racetrack to watch horse and dog racing. Daytona Beach hosts a popular NASCAR race called the Daytona 500 every February. Floridians sun themselves on sandy, coastal beaches. They also get in the water to swim, surf, and snorkel. Fishers head to lakes and rivers to catch largemouth bass and catfish.

fun fact

Jai alai is a popular sport in Florida. It is similar to handball. Players attach a 2-foot (61-centimeter) basket to their arm. They use this to catch and throw the ball against the wall.

Daytona 500

Key Lime Pie

Ingredients:

1 unbaked graham cracker pie shell

1 14-ounce can sweetened condensed milk

3 egg yolks, beaten

1/2 cup key lime juice
(If you can't find key lime juice, regular lime juice is okay.)

Directions:

1. Preheat oven to 375°F.

2. Combine egg yolks, sweetened condensed milk, and lime juice. Mix well.

3. Pour into pie shell. Bake for 15 minutes. Let cool.

4. Top with whipped cream and lime slices.

shrimp and grits

Cuban sandwich

Florida **cuisine** features many influences from Latin American countries. Tampa claims to have invented the Cuban sandwich. Ham, roast pork, and salami sit between Cuban bread. Swiss cheese, mustard, and slices of dill pickles top the meats.

Some Floridian cuisine is called "Floribbean." This type of food combines dishes and flavors from Caribbean countries. Key lime pies were first made in the Florida Keys. The pies are made using juice from the tiny limes grown on these islands. Key West is known for its conch fritters. The meat of conch shellfish is coated in batter and fried to make these tasty treats.

23

Festivals

Every January, the Gasparilla Pirate Festival invades Tampa. Ye Mystic Krewe of Gasparilla sails into Tampa's Hillsborough Bay aboard a pirate ship. Pretend pirates and people of Tampa come together to enjoy a pirate parade and street festival.

Thousands of people gather in Miami for the Orange Bowl Festival and college football game in January. The festival includes a tennis tournament and sailboat race. Miami's Little Havana hosts the Calle Ocho Festival each March. Attendees can taste Cuban food and hear musicians perform *salsa* and *merengue* hits.

fun fact

In 1998, the world's longest conga line was formed at the Calle Ocho Festival. Now this festival is in the Guinness Book of World Records!

Gasparilla Pirate Festival

Little Havana

Did you know?

Little Haiti and Little Managua are other Miami neighborhoods. People who have come from Haiti and Nicaragua make their homes in these areas.

During the 1960s, thousands of Cuban people moved to Miami. They left Cuba because they disagreed with its government. Many of these Cubans settled near Miami's Eighth Street, or *Calle Ocho*. This area is now known as Little Havana because of all of the Cubans who live there.

A walk down Little Havana's streets takes people past shops that sell Cuban products. Restaurants along *Calle Ocho* serve Cuba's famous coffee. In Domino Park, old men gather for competitive games of dominoes. This thriving neighborhood shows Florida's appreciation for the **diverse** cultures of its residents.

Fast Facts About Florida

Florida's Flag

Florida's flag has a white background with a red X. At the center of the X is the state seal. The seal shows a ship at sea sailing on shining ocean waters. A Native American woman stands on shore with some palm trees. The state's name and motto are also included on the seal.

State Flower
orange blossom

State Nicknames:	The Sunshine State The Alligator State The Everglades State
State Motto:	"In God We Trust"
Year of Statehood:	1845
Capital City:	Tallahassee
Other Major Cities:	Jacksonville, Miami, Tampa
Population:	18,801,310 (2010)
Area:	58,976 square miles (152,747 square kilometers); Florida is the 22nd largest state.
Major Industries:	farming, tourism, food processing, electronics
Natural Resources:	water, forests, phosphate, limestone
State Government:	120 representatives; 40 senators
Federal Government:	27 representatives; 2 senators
Electoral Votes:	29

State Bird
northern mockingbird

State Animal
Florida panther

Glossary

archipelago—a chain of islands

citrus fruits—fruits with thick skins and pulpy insides

Civil War—a war between the northern (Union) and southern (Confederate) states that lasted from 1861 to 1865

Confederacy—the group of southern states that formed a new country in the early 1860s; they fought against the northern states during the Civil War.

coral—small ocean animals whose skeletons make up coral reefs

coral reefs—structures made of coral that usually grow in shallow seawater

cuisine—a style of cooking unique to a certain area or group of people

diverse—made up of people from many different backgrounds

endangered—at risk of becoming extinct

groves—areas in which fruit trees are planted

gulf—part of an ocean or sea that extends into land

marshes—wetlands with grasses and plants

native—originally from a specific place

panhandle—a narrow stretch of land attached to a larger piece of land

peninsula—a section of land that extends out from a larger piece of land and is almost completely surrounded by water

plains—large areas of flat land

resorts—vacation spots that offer recreation, entertainment, and relaxation

saw grass—tall grass-like plants with sharp, saw-like edges

service jobs—jobs that perform tasks for people or businesses

straits—narrow stretches of water that connect two larger bodies of water

subtropical—having hot, humid weather

tourist—a person who travels to visit another place

To Learn More

AT THE LIBRARY

Bullard, Lisa. *The Everglades*. Minneapolis, Minn.: Lerner Publications Co., 2010.

Kelley, K.C. *Miami Heat*. Mankato, Minn.: Child's World, 2013.

Lourie, Peter. *The Manatee Scientists: Saving Vulnerable Species*. Boston, Mass.: Houghton Mifflin Books for Children, 2011.

ON THE WEB

Learning more about Florida is as easy as 1, 2, 3.

1. Go to www.factsurfer.com.

2. Enter "Florida" into the search box.

3. Click the "Surf" button and you will see a list of related Web sites.

With factsurfer.com, finding more information is just a click away.

Index

The images in this book are reproduced through the courtesy of: Mariia Sats, front cover (bottom); David Osborn/ Alamy, p. 6; (Collection)/ Prints & Photographs Division/ Library of Congress, p. 7 (left); Everett Collection/ SuperStock, p. 7 (middle); Associated Press, p. 7 (right); Bertl123, p. 8 (top); inga spence/ Alamy, p. 8 (bottom); fotomak, pp. 8-9, 16-17; North Wind Picture Archives/ Alamy, p. 10; Juan Carlos Munoz/ Age Fotostock/ SuperStock, pp. 10-11; Stocktrek Images/ SuperStock, pp. 12-13; Arto Hakola, p. 13 (top); Gerald A. DeBoer, p. 13 (middle); Image Source/ Glow Images, p. 13 (bottom); Gary I. Rothstein/ EPA/ Newscom, p. 14 (top); James Schwabel/ Age Fotostock/ SuperStock, p. 14 (bottom); Ian Dagnall/ Alamy, p. 15; Richard Cavalleri, p. 17; Bloomberg/ Getty Images, p. 18; Pam McLean/ Getty Images, p. 19; Associated Press/ J. Pat Carter, p. 20; Associated Press/ Autostock, Russell LaBounty, pp. 20-21; Darren K. Fisher, p. 22; msheldrake, p. 23 (top); REDAV, p. 23 (bottom); Alexander Tamargo/ Getty Images, p. 24; Associated Press/ Ron Williams, pp. 24-25; Mary Kent/ Alamy, pp. 26-27; Alvaro Leiva/ Age Fotostock/ SuperStock, p. 27; Pakmor, p. 28 (top); ANCH, p. 28 (bottom); Matt Knoth, p. 29 (left); Animals Animals/ SuperStock, p. 29 (right).